SAVING SEEDS

Saving Seeds

A HOME GARDENER'S GUIDE TO PRESERVING PLANT BIODIVERSITY

DAN JASON

HARBOUR
PUBLISHING

Harbour Publishing Co. Ltd.

P.O. Box 219, Madeira Park, BC, V0N 2H0

www.harbourpublishing.com

Cover and text design by Shed Simas / Onça Design
Printed and bound in Canada
Printed on 100% recycled paper
All cover images by Karen Mouat except: lentils, Adobe Stock / bahrialtay;
corn, Adobe Stock / Ozgur Coskun; pumpkin seeds, Adobe Stock / Picture Partners;
sunflower seeds, Adobe Stock / igorkol_ter

Harbour Publishing acknowledges the support of the Canada Council for the Arts, which last year invested $153 million to bring the arts to Canadians throughout the country.

Nous remercions le Conseil des arts du Canada de son soutien. L'an dernier, le Conseil a investi 153 millions de dollars pour mettre de l'art dans la vie des Canadiennes et des Canadiens de tout le pays.

We also gratefully acknowledge financial support from the Government of Canada and from the Province of British Columbia through the BC Arts Council.

Library and Archives Canada Cataloguing in Publication

Title: Saving seeds : a home gardener's guide to preserving plant biodiversity / Dan Jason.
Names: Jason, Dan, author.
Identifiers: Canadiana (print) 20190222069 | Canadiana (ebook) 20190222107 |
      ISBN 9781550179002 (softcover) | ISBN 9781550179019 (HTML)
Subjects: LCSH: Seeds. | LCSH: Seeds—Harvesting. | LCSH: Seeds—Storage.
Classification: LCC SB118.3 .J37 2020 | DDC 631.5/21—dc23

TABLE OF CONTENTS

FOREWORD:
A GUIDE

THIS BOOK IS DIVIDED into four parts, all part and parcel of my urging you to partake in the responsibility and the joy of saving seeds.

Part 1 is a personal overview of how seed affairs have become what they are. This section encapsulates over 30 years of observing the seed world while participating in it as a mail order seed company.

Part 2 outlines some thoughts I now have about seeds and some of the background experiences that led to those thoughts. I'm hoping this section excites you to the possibilities of what might be in store for you if you take the Seedy Road.

Part 3 is an initial guide to saving seeds. Saving seeds is simple, easy and straightforward.

Part 4 lets you know that the revitalization of seeds is already a social movement. Beyond actually growing seeds, there are many ways to participate effectively in the preservation of our seed heritage.

PART 1

Our Challenge and Opportunity

FORTY YEARS AGO, I was just a backyard gardener living on Salt Spring Island, between Vancouver Island and mainland British Columbia. I had the opportunity to grow food on a few acres of fertile land that belonged to The Salt Spring Centre of Yoga. Because they provide vegetarian meals for residents and visitors, I experimented with growing substantial food crops such as beans and grains. After a few years, I was excitedly growing many crops that aren't usually found in seed catalogues. I started my own mail order seed company, Salt Spring Seeds, in 1986.

As I immersed myself in seeds, I was naturally enough observing what was going on in larger seed spheres. Looking back over just a few decades, it's hard to believe how fast things have changed.

In the mid-1980s, the Canadian and US governments had crop research stations across the continent and some quite substantial gene banks preserving our seed heritage. Plant scientists sought to develop locally adapted seeds for disease and pest resistance, better nutrition, higher yield and earliness. Such research was done to benefit both farmers and consumers. Information about the seeds and the seeds themselves were shared with pride as part of a long-standing tradition. It went without saying that an important function of government was researching and maintaining the best agricultural crops.

Now the seed situation is totally different. Gene banks and research stations have been downsized and neglected. American and Canadian governments have handed over seed research and development to transnational corporations with totally different agendas for seeds.

Corporate mergers of seed growers have accelerated at such a pace that there are now only a few giant rulers. Patented seeds have become common in catalogues. Plants that have always belonged to everyone are now "owned" by corporations. Farmers are being taken to court for saving seed.

Millions of acres of farmland are being planted with altered seed that has had genes from other life forms inserted. The majority of processed and animal food products in North America are derived from genetically modified (GMO) seeds.

Research in corporate and university laboratories is now about not good food but what I would call "bad" food.

About 25 years ago, the biotech people were starting to claim that GMO seeds would grow more nutritious food, would result in lower pesticide and herbicide use and would help feed the planet. I scoffed at such promises, although part of me thought they would probably try to improve some crops nutritionally, work on disease resistance or shorten maturity times. That hasn't happened, however. The history of the genetic engineering of seeds, of inserting genes from totally different species into seeds, is a monotonous and uninspiring one. Virtually all corporate genetic seed modifications have aimed to make plants resistant to weed and bug killers.

I consider GMO food bad food because it's designed with poison in mind. If you create plants that do not succumb to herbicides, pesticides and fungicides, then the nature of what we're consuming is all wrapped up in poison. Tinkering with genes from totally different species and mixing them up in our food has never been done before and has potentially deadly consequences. Yet it is being done with little testing, no consultation and no notification.

The promise that genetic engineering would reduce use of agricultural poisons was dubious back then. Now it's quite horrific how, with the increased use of herbicides, weeds have adapted to become superweeds that nothing can control. It's also been appalling to me how genetically engineered crops have contaminated the crops of farmers trying to grow clean, healthy food.

I sometimes try to grasp the immense power of those who push GMO crops on us. Most GMO crops have been dismal failures resulting in cardboard tomatoes, spuds that are duds and inferior cotton. Most GMO companies have been unable to stay in business, yet the ones that remain seem to call all the shots with food. In both Canada and the United States, huge majorities of people want to have products from GMO seeds labelled as such, yet nothing much happens.

Terminator seeds followed on the heels of GMO seeds as part of the arsenal of corporate agribusiness promising hope for the future. Terminator seeds have been genetically altered so that plants don't produce viable seeds. They more transparently reveal the name of the game to be profit and control. Such seeds threaten the livelihoods of all farmers who save their own seed. That minds would design seeds to terminate themselves is incomprehensible to most people, and there was enough outraged reaction that experiments were stopped. Yet, in 2005, Canada tried to overturn the international moratorium on the research and development of seeds that are engineered to self-destruct. Fortunately, the ban was upheld the next year.

Equally incomprehensible and sinister have been attempts (mostly successful) in the past few years economically to blackmail countries with starving populations into accepting GMO food as "aid."

When I started out as a seed farmer, the seeds for our major food crops were not owned by anyone in particular. In fact, until that recently it didn't even occur to most people, including myself, that seeds could be owned at all. It's one thing to claim ownership of seeds substantially altered through hybridization or genetic engineering. Now corporations are brazenly claiming exclusive ownership of seeds that have been in the public domain for thousands of years, such as chapati wheat or basmati rice.

Control of resources has always been the essence of the game for those bent on political power. If you own the oil, the water, the minerals, the land, then you own the people too. However, owning seeds in the manner it's happening now is unprecedented.

Who is planning for the fallout from the explosions of corporate monomania? Who is saving seeds and guarding our food supply for the future? Are there people giving thought to what might happen if a bird flu pandemic wipes out chicken dinner or if mad cow disease spells the end of steaks and burgers? Are elected representatives planning for the time when it becomes too costly to transport food thousands of miles or to grow food with petroleum-driven machinery and petroleum-based biocides? Is anybody thinking about what will happen when we can't drive to a store or restaurant?

Such a time might be very close and, for many people, has already arrived. Disasters are not going to end for a while, and not unless we respect the fragile balance of living systems. If we don't wake up and work together for everyone's common good, it may soon be too late.

An agriculture that promotes chemical monoculture cannot work for very long. In North America, it worked for the second half of the twentieth century because there was a deep bank of soil, plus trees to hold water and stabilize the weather. Now trees are gone, soil has eroded, wells are empty and the weather is predictable only in its unpredictability.

The task of reinventing agriculture is a necessary and crucial one. Probably the most meaningful endeavour for humanity at this time is replanting the global garden. Without a massive international effort to reduce greenhouse gases, stabilize climate change and stop the decline of the earth's life support systems by using plants, all other good struggles will be overtaken by ecological chaos.

Can we stop buying into processes and products that are designed only for the corporate bottom line before it becomes impossible not to? Why should food be so wrapped up with money? There is already a vast surplus of whole grains and beans being grown in North America. Why shouldn't food be a right instead of a privilege? Much evidence shows we can all be well fed.

Why not encourage people to have a rewarding livelihood by farming the richness of the earth, to live on the land and derive satisfaction and fulfillment from the infinite beauty and entertainment of nature? Why not start to realize the vast potential for growing food within our urban environments?

What about the thought that I hear expressed by many people these days—"The earth is pretty messed up but it's still likely the most incredible place in the universe"? Why should the tiniest proportion of people have all the power and resources? Why don't we go for it and try to use all our smarts for mutual benefit? Why not create a place where all life is honoured and cherished?

Seeds are perhaps the most potent beginning point we have now. They can light the way to growing high-quality crops that are not dependent on unsustainable herbicides and pesticides. They have the power to feed, clothe and shelter us. They have the power to clean our air and water. The threat of their extermination must rally us to their protection, preservation, enhancement and multiplication. For seeds to remain public treasures, we must embrace them and create agendas for them that are people oriented rather than power oriented.

Saving seeds was once an eloquently simple process. Seeds belonged to everyone in a sacred sort of way. The confused mindset that inserts foreign genes into seeds, that patents and kills seeds, is one that would destroy the very garden that feeds us.

Industrial agriculture is not going to preserve our priceless treasure of seeds. Nor is there much chance of getting governments to return to the custodianship of our food heritage. That leaves millions of backyard growers and small-scale farmers, people who truly love plants, to hand them on to the next generation.

The seeds that will sustain us are the ones that can be easily and joyfully saved by anyone who is reading these words.

PART 2

Let's Hear It for Seeds!

IN MY 40 YEARS OF GARDENING, seeds have expanded my horizons in so many ways. Before going on to the practical aspects of seed saving, I wish to share a few seedy thoughts, along with some of the background to those thoughts. Hurray for seeds—mentors of mine in the realms of acceptance, enjoyment and enthusiasm!

SEEDS INVENT US NO LESS THAN LANGUAGE, SEWING TOGETHER THE FABRIC OF THE WORLDS WE WEAR.

I studied anthropology and languages in university and came to see how our language does indeed shape the way we see the world. Seeds too, as I've come to realize, affect us in myriad ways. Seed alchemy creates the clothes we wear, the buildings we inhabit, the meals we prepare and the lives we live.

I often feel on a personal level that, in a strange yet totally familiar way, seeds have indeed invented me. I grew up in the suburbs of Montreal in the 1950s at a time when no one grew anything but ornamentals around their houses. I had a totally compelling urge to dig up our back lawn and plant vegetables. Year after year I pestered my parents to let me make a garden. Finally they said OK. Now I remember the little two-by-three-foot (60 cm × 90 cm) area under our back porch as the garden that seeded all my gardens since. I still laugh when I remember showing my aunt the beautiful carrots that came out of that little patch of dirt and her telling me she thought that carrots grew on trees.

When I was about 12, I happened one day to notice a seed catalogue that had somehow come in our mail. I have such a

Carrot (*Daucus carota* subsp. *sativus*)

full memory of picking up that catalogue, transfixed in a sense by something I already knew but for which I had no words. Now, after over 30 annual catalogues of my own, I know a little of what that feeling is about and I have more words for it!

THE STORIES OF SEEDS ARE THE STORIES OF US ALL.

Seeds are a lot like us in many ways. In some respects, we *are* seeds. By growing and eating them, directly or indirectly, we are carrying them and ourselves forward into our next sowings and harvests, our next selves.

We all know that there are good years and bad years. What neither organic manuals nor chemical farming texts will tell you, however, is that sometimes the good or bad seed seasons have nothing whatsoever to do with what you can figure out. Sometimes no amount of NPK fertilizer or compost can explain health or disease in plants any more than amounts of exercise or vitamins can explain health or disease in humans.

I offer you three personal examples of how time and place can create a unique energy.

A few years ago my peppers were unbelievably fabulous. Plants were laden with ripe beauties well into November.

Many of my gardening cohorts around here were similarly amazed by unprecedented pepper production.

The year before that tomato blight hit all of us here on Salt Spring on July 15. However, the tomatoes didn't succumb to become blackened mush in a few days but went on to bear many unblemished fruits.

About a dozen years ago, I received from a First Nations site some tobacco seed that had been stored dry enough to still be viable after a thousand years. (It had been carbon dated.) Even though I planted the tobacco plants in fairly inconspicuous spots, they accosted visitors like nothing else in the garden. "The sense of something from another time" was how a few people worded it. I continue to be struck by how these 1,000-year-old tobacco plants convey something very different from anything else in the garden.

The above three examples involve significant seed saving choices bound to be invisible to corporate or federal scientists. They wouldn't be interested in the tobacco because tobacco is now a much larger plant that has been bred to be processed with dozens of toxic additives. They wouldn't be interested in the tomatoes, although it's quite possible those seeds might carry some inbuilt protection against future blight. They wouldn't consider that a vintage year for pepper seed might be especially significant for future plantings.

Are the seeds that we will carry to next year going to tell stories of human interaction with the earth, the hoeings and the weedings, the waterings and the gleanings, or will they carry the resonance of huge machinery and pursuit of profit? It seems quite certain that seasons are not going to smile on harvests of plenty as they used to. Hurricanes, floods, drought and earthquakes are going to wipe out food and seed harvests unless many people in many places are providing food security. We can transcend inevitable crop disasters by backing each other up through years fat and thin.

SEEDS LEND US EARS TO HEAR THE WINDS OF ALL THOSE MUTUAL JOURNEYS OF SEED TO SEED.

Speaking of good years and bad years, through most of my gardening life I've never been able to grow good carrots. Nothing has ever matched the presence of my first carrots grown under our back porch when I was 10. This past year was different. As my brother would say, "Finally, the kid, 50 years later, grows good carrots again!"

Seeds sprout and grow plants through the seasons until it's time to do it all over again. The love a seed saver bestows on seeds is the same love that rides the windy merry-go-round of watchfulness and waiting, pain and endurance, hope and happiness.

THE FORESTS OF TREES WHOSE BREATH WE BREATHE WERE ALL ONCE SEEDS.

Sometimes I'm in my garden and look at the soil and think of all the compost I've added, the mulch I've put down, the cover crops I've turned under. Then when I look over the fence to the huge firs and cedars beyond, I think of all the flowers or veggies I've grown and how tiny they are compared with the trees! No one was doing anything to the soil the trees grew in and yet they grew up to the sky.

I'm living in a forest as I write this and the air around here is very energizing. I know how lucky I am. A lot of our planet has been denuded of trees. Much more attention is paid to using what's left than to planting for the future. Yet even in arid places, if rainwater can be held for a while instead of draining away, certain trees can shoot up a few feet in a season and many more feet in another. Those trees can shade the soil, nurse other trees and have fruits and vegetables growing around them. In two or three years, bountiful gardens can be growing and growing.

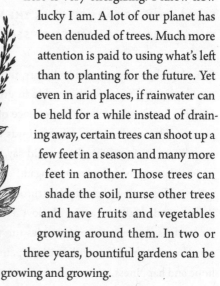

SUCH EYES SEEDS ARE, OPENING US TO THE SEEDY WORLDS OF BIRDS AND BEES AND BUTTERFLIES.

I've had such diverse gardens over the years because of growing hundreds of different things for Salt Spring Seeds. I am amazed how the more things you grow, the more birds, bees and butterflies show up. Flowers and the seeds that follow host an unbelievable amount of activity. When it comes time for the seed saver to gather the seeds and spread them to dry, she or he is bound to notice that a lot of homes have been destroyed in the process. As soon as you look at the seeds on the tray, you notice that there are thousands of little insects all scurrying away from the light. Every plant species has different bugs. What's really amazing is how they magically appear out of nowhere when you start to grow a different flower.

In all my years of growing gardens, bugs and birds have never bugged me. (Except once the ravens mixed up my bean seeds before I could poke them in the ground!) I've always found that diversity works for everyone's benefit.

LET US REPEAT THE VITAL STATISTICS OF SEEDS THE WAY WE DO FOR MOVIE STARS AND SPORTS HEROES.

I want to vouch that learning seed statistics is both fun and inspiring. In my teens, I could give you numbers for batting averages and home runs hit, goals scored and penalty minutes, touchdown passes and catches. When I was in my twenties, I could tell you about scores of movies, actors and directors. It feels to me now a much sweeter and rewarding intimacy to know seed details than to keep up with someone else's antics with a wooden stick or pigskin football or rubber puck.

What does this mean in reality? I know, for example, that Black Coco beans are more than twice the size of Black Turtle beans. Still, Black Cocos normally yield less than Black Turtles in terms of weight of dry bean per plant. Yet there's something special about having those big black beans in certain dishes that overrides their lower yield. It's their slightly more chocolate flavour as well as the visual boost they give to soups and stews that keeps me growing them.

Corporate agriculture would give you one tomato, a tomato that still looks fresh three weeks after it was put on the supermarket shelf. But what about those Brandywine tomatoes, one slice of which turns a sandwich into a feast, or those clusters of cherry tomatoes that make for bright-eyed salads or invigorating snacks in the garden? What about tomatoes that make superior sauces or the ones that are best for freezing or drying? What about the vital statistics of orange, yellow, white, purple and black tomatoes that delight the eye as well as the palate?

THE CORNUCOPIA OF FOODS AND HERBS AND SPICES REFLECTS OUR OWN IMMENSITY.

In 1993, I was privileged to travel to Ethiopia and observe farming traditions that had gone on for countless generations. By then, I had already acquired and grown out many different seeds from around the world. I remember the feeling of pride I had when I told some plant scientists in the gene bank in Addis Ababa that I had grown Ethiopian barley. "Which one?" they laughed. Then they told me that they had close to 6,000 acquisitions of barley in that very building. "We have barleys that we like to eat in the morning and barleys we prefer in the evening, we have barleys for special occasions, we have barleys for sprouting, barleys for baking, barleys for thatching, barleys for making beer and barleys we only feed to animals."

I remember the lights going on for me with the realization that "fast food" North Americans

Barley
(*Hordeum vulgare*)

like myself can hardly appreciate the agricultural and culinary depth of other cultures. Now, two dozen years later, I'm starting to believe we have a good chance of embracing much more of the immensity of world food traditions. After all, when it comes down to it, of all the things one might try to acquire, good food for every meal has got to rank pretty high. Eating can be associated with so much pleasure and enjoyment. That's part of what the Slow Food Movement, founded in Italy in the late 1980s, is all about. It's now a nationwide movement in over 160 countries. Millions of people are opting to commune at meals rather than gulp them down.

For me, one of the core concepts here is whole food. Cooking barley or wheat whole instead of pearling or grinding the kernels does create a slowed-down eating experience. You cannot eat whole grains as quickly as toast or crackers. On the other hand, because you have to chew each mouthful, you get to think about the fact that you're eating and you get to be a little more relaxed about it all. Also you get to eat your vitamins and minerals instead of having to take supplements.

Gardeners know that some varieties of fruits and vegetables are simply better than others for their flavour, health and productivity. They know that ripe and fresh is best and they can intimately appreciate degrees of ripeness and freshness.

A lot of people, growers included, have no idea how significant variety is for dry beans and whole grains. It's also little known that beans and grains change significantly as they age. Beans that have been sitting in bins for months or years lose their lustre, take much longer to cook and are much harder to digest than beans that have been recently harvested.

One of the foods I've been trying to promote over the years is whole soybeans. I have some black, brown and bicoloured cultivars that have always matured for me here in the Pacific Northwest. They cook up in 90 minutes, never cause indigestion and are as flavourful as any baking bean. They are so high in fat and protein that a small amount in a meal makes that meal feel very substantial.

In terms of soybean cultivation, what we have right now in North America is millions of acres of GMO soybeans and not much else. The most popular cultivar, Roundup Ready soybeans, is a yellow bean that takes days to cook and is still indigestible. Instead, the majority of these soybeans are ground up for animal feed or processed into food products. As the name suggests, Roundup Ready soybeans have been engineered to withstand Roundup, a poison that kills pretty much all green growth. (Some studies have found it to kill tadpoles and frogs as well, and experiments have suggested serious effects on human stomachs.) Roundup Ready soybeans are processed into dozens of food and industrial products, including soybean oil, lecithin, soy milk and tofu. There's no doubt we have more sustainable options to explore than Roundup Ready soybeans and other GMO crops.

SEEDS—LIKE PEOPLE, IF YOU GIVE THEM HALF A CHANCE—FIND PLACES TO SPROUT AND THRIVE.

Common bean
(*Phaseolus vulgaris*)

I have a gorgeous red-and-white pole bean called Aunt Jean's Bean that was sent to me by her niece in the early days of my seed company. Aunt Jean had grown it in Saskatchewan for many decades before giving up her farm. Recently, similar beans were mailed to me from England and Australia. Over several years, I compared the size of the beans, the number of beans per pod and the number of pods to a plant, as well as their taste and texture. I concluded that they were indeed the same bean. That bean has done some good hitchhiking. Where did it start out in the first place?

Every year more seeds find their way to me. In a year or two many of them are popping up by themselves in my garden in such a friendly sort of way.

A DIVERSITY OF PEOPLE GROWING A DIVERSITY OF CROPS IS OUR BEST BET FOR ABUNDANCE.

These years, it is common for most places to set new records for rain, wind, drought, heat and cold.

Four years ago, it didn't stop raining here on Salt Spring Island until July 15. That was the day many tomato growers got hit with blight. It didn't rain again for months and most tomatoes survived. If I hadn't planted a cultivar I obtained from Nigeria along with the rest of the 200 tomatoes I was growing, I never would have discovered that, unlike many similar tomatoes, it was totally blight resistant.

When a disease hit barley crops worldwide in the '70s, it was a cultivar from Ethiopia that enabled government breeders to develop resistant varieties.

Governments are no longer researching appropriate crops that can adapt to these changing times. Seeds in national gene banks often don't germinate. Corporations are fixated on plants that withstand poison.

We don't need to insert genes from other species into our seeds to assure our future. Thousands of fantastic varieties of roots, fruits, greens and herbs still exist thanks to generation after generation of good seed work. We have the exciting opportunity to make more of these our own than ever before. It's crucial to grow out lots of crops annually, to maintain living gene banks far and wide, to observe how our food and medicinal crops perform in these changing environmental conditions and to have systems in place to exchange seeds and information.

MONEY IS NOT AN ISSUE.

As a grassroots movement rises to preserve and enhance our agricultural heritage, we will see that no huge grants, elaborate scientific equipment or expensive laboratories will be required. Seeds already exist to fulfill our needs, now and in the future. We can do what seed collectors have done for 10,000 years. We can save seeds. We can also be there to take new seed offerings from Mother Nature and to hybridize seeds without perverting them. After every growing season, we can compare notes freely without patenting our seeds or our information. We can talk or write to each other, we can email each other, we can support each other and we can exchange seeds knowing that it's not about money.

SEEDS ARE OUR WINDOWS AND OUR WINGS TO FUTURE SELVES, TO FUTURE, UNIMAGINABLE EXTRAVAGANZAS OF PLANTS AND PEOPLE.

I have a plant in my garden called Magenta Spreen, which I've allowed to naturalize. I also harvest seed from it. A plant person named Alan Kapuler developed it through traditional breeding methods. He took the common lamb's quarters plant and by selecting for the light-pink blush that sometimes appears at the base of the leaves, he got a plant that always has a strong magenta heart around the stalk. The sight of this plant in my garden has a very different effect on me than seeing its ordinary relative that most growers consider a weed. It radiates a vibrancy that often perks me up. I'm much more likely to put it in my salads than I am the regular lamb's quarters. People I introduce to it are also quite delighted by it.

Alan Kapuler also bred Rainbow Inca corn by judicious crossings of many heritage varieties. Each cob of this corn has the beautiful colours of old flour corns but it is nonetheless the kind of corn we eat off the cob. It is sweet but still has a lot more nutrition than today's supersweet corns that are all glucose.

About 10 years ago, an apprentice of mine spotted two plants in a row of regular green beans that had iridescent pink pods. I grew them out and they've stayed true to their amazing colour ever since. I've never seen anything like Tanya's Pink Pod bean in all my bean explorations. They are great snap beans that keep their succulent texture a long time and they elicit appreciative wonder when you see them with normal green and wax beans.

Lamb's quarters
(*Chenopodium album*)

Although I maintain over 100 varieties of lettuce, I had never seen cultivars cross until 2004. That year

I was growing a variety of butter lettuce that had maroon dots splashed on the green leaves. I was also growing lots of oak leaf lettuces. When I grew out the seeds from the one oak leaf with dark speckles that appeared in 2005, it happily stayed true. It is now part of the Salt Spring Seeds catalogue as Mottled Looseleaf.

Most gardeners love the experience of eating what they've been watching and tending for weeks and months. What is being imbibed is not just food as such but also the beauty of all those moments of being present with the plants.

The attentive seed saver can expand such full appreciation to include future gardens and meals. Nature often gifts possibilities for new gardens and we can choose them for our sustenance and delight.

SEEDS EMPOWER US TO TAKE PERSONAL RESPONSIBILITY FOR OUR LIVES.

At this moment small-scale agriculture is threatened to its very roots. The last thing corporations want is people who won't buy their products because they grow their own food, medicine and seeds. Industrial agriculture, even as it starts to disintegrate, is trying to wipe small growers off the map. Hellish diseases are being created by hellish factory farming conditions, yet small growers are told they must kill their animals or birds to protect us all from the likes of mad cow disease or bird flu.

Where I live, in a small agricultural community, regulations are coming into effect making it economically impossible for farmers to continue a long-standing and problem-free tradition of raising cows, goats, sheep and chickens. Corporations are also trying to push their own exclusive monopoly of foods, herbs and seeds through intense government lobbying.

It's a weird state of affairs when people who grow their own food and medicine are treated like criminals. This cannot last very much longer, however, as the natural consequences of total-control agriculture increasingly take their toll on our bodies, our land and our economies.

There are so many powerful herbs that can make up one's living medicine chest. One of the strongest for me has been one of the most striking plants you can grow. Milk thistle has rich white patterns on its large barbed, bright-green leaves.

Some years ago, a friend was dying of stomach and liver cancer and was told he had only a few weeks to live. He had read that milk thistle seeds could help regenerate the liver and asked me if I had any seeds. Milk thistle, back then, wasn't one of my notable plants but I did have lots of seed. He started seriously chewing on those seeds. I'll never forget the look on his face when he told me he could digest food again. Frank lived many more months and milk thistle is now definitely among my favourite plants.

If you grow and save the seed of your own food and medicine you grow your own health and abundance. The fact that those seeds can carry you right round again year after year means there's no expiry date when you'll have to shell out money once more.

Beyond the security that comes from self-reliance, there's another kind of empowerment that comes to the seed saver directly through the seeds. Every seed saver I know attests to an uplifting and energizing feeling that comes from working with seeds. Whether it be munching flax seeds right off the plant, pouring poppy seeds out of their seed heads, imbibing the incredible aroma of lavender as you rub the stalks to release the seeds or opening the pods of beans to see their gorgeous colours and patterns, seed saving will vitalize you no end.

Milk thistle
(*Silybum marianum*)

PART 3

How to Save Seeds

I THINK THE PRACTICE of lots of people saving seeds is due for a revival. Seed saving is rewarding in so many ways. It's very easy. If you find yourself smitten by it, there are ways you can get more expert about it. However, even a little seed saving is an empowering and powerful thing to do.

BASICS

What you basically do when you save seeds is this: you go to the seeds when they are ready and get them, you make sure they're really dry and then you store them.

It's as simple as that but...

Getting good seeds at the right time involves knowing the usual life cycle of a plant and whether a seed will stay true.

You can gather them in different ways such as plucking, rubbing, shaking or grabbing. Ways of harvesting are often quickly obvious but not always.

Making sure seeds are dry enough means having a good drying space for them.

Storing seeds well involves having appropriate labels and containers for them.

PLANT TYPES AND SPECIFICS

Plants are annual, biennial or perennial.

Annual plants (such as lettuce and tomatoes) flower and mature seed in the same year.

Biennial plants (such as carrots and beets) are normally harvested as food in their first summer or fall but do not flower or produce seed until the next year. In mild coastal or southern areas, biennials will survive the winter under a cover of hay or leaves. In most of continental North America, biennials must be dug up and carefully stored elsewhere during the winter to be replanted in the spring. Most biennials become tall and bushy when going to seed, taking up more space than they did the previous year. They can be thinned or transplanted to twice the usual spacing.

Perennial plants live and bear seed year after year.

Plants are also classified as either self-pollinating or cross-pollinated, although sometimes they can be both.

Self-pollinating plants: Pollen is not transferred from one flower to another, either on the same plant or between plants. The process occurs within each flower. The flowers have both male and female plant parts and pollination occurs successfully within the single bloom. The seeds of these plants almost always retain the quality of the parent seed, or stay "true." Because they rarely cross with another variety of the same species, isolating them is unnecessary unless you want absolute purity in a strain.

Cross-pollinated plants: The pollen from one flower fertilizes another flower, either on the same or another plant. Either wind or insects carry the pollen. It is important to know the other varieties of the same species with which a plant has the potential to exchange pollen. For example, if your cabbage and your broccoli flower at the same time, the seed will primarily produce plants that look like neither parent. Allowing only one variety of each potentially cross-pollinated vegetable to flower out eliminates the need to separate plants from each other. As well, barriers can be erected or planted, plantings can be staggered or crops can be covered with garden fabric.

Following are the seed stories for most potential seed crops in your garden. They are the self-pollinating annuals, the cross-pollinated annuals, the cross-pollinated biennials and the perennials.

SELF-POLLINATING ANNUALS

These include lettuces, beans, grains, tomatoes and peppers. It is easy to save a diversity of them and they are very significant crops to save.

LETTUCE

Lettuces are unusual in the manner that they complete their cycle and go to seed. They don't dry down but instead they grow up. They put up a flowering stalk that can reach waist-high, and as they do so the leaves become shrunken versions of their former selves. The candelabra-like appearance of many cultivars is so attractive that their aesthetic appeal could be taken into consideration when planning your garden.

A single lettuce can produce hundreds of small yellow flowers atop its stalk. The flowers become bunches of feathery little seed sites, each flower creating 8 to 15 seeds. The seeds are a miniature version of dandelion seeds, having a tiny parachute perfect for riding the breezes. They are little wedges about an eighth of an inch (0.31 cm) long and are either white or dark, depending on variety.

Someone wanting to have enough seed for the coming year could simply pluck two or three fuzzy seed heads to get a couple dozen seeds.

The seeds ripen over several weeks: when they start to appear there are many flowers still blooming. If you want a lot, it's best to wait until a third of the seeds are ready and collect them when conditions are as dry as possible.

The plants can be tipped into whatever container you're employing and shaken to release the seeds. You can also rub the seed heads between the thumb and forefinger of one hand while holding the bucket or bag under them with the other. I've found the plastic pails that are usually available from stores that sell ice cream cones to be perfect for gathering lots of different seeds: seed heads can be easily bent into them and shaken against the sides.

After harvest, lettuce seeds are best dried for another day or two. Spread them out on plates, pans, trays or bucket lids in a warm, airy place. The freshly gathered seed usually comes with a little fluff and flower parts. The fluff quickly dries in the presence of heat and any little bugs you may have picked with the seeds will usually disappear in a few hours.

The seed can be rubbed between the fingers to release the fluff. Most of the fluff can be blown away if you're careful not to blow too hard. Sifting it through an appropriate screen can also clean the seed. For the amateur seed saver, it is not crucial for the seeds to be totally clean, just totally dry.

It's wise to have identifying labels accompanying the seeds at each step and to put sticky labels on their containers.

Romaine lettuce
(*Lactuca sativa* var. *longifolia*)

Lettuce seeds take up little space. It's easy to find small glass or plastic containers for them. Film canisters and small plastic bags also work well.

Lettuce seed is usually collected in September and October. If you want to be a saver of lettuce seed, it's best to find those cultivars that produce the kind of lettuce you like but also produce seed before the plants are frozen or rained out. In short-season growing areas, it might be necessary to start lettuces early indoors.

Lettuces rarely cross but it's best not to allow undomesticated lettuce varieties, such as wild or prickly lettuce, to flower nearby.

If you start saving lettuces you'll be amazed by the wonderful shapes, textures and colours of the leaves, plus all the diverse ways the flowering stalks shoot up. Lettuce seeds keep a high viability for at least four years.

TOMATOES

Tomatoes are the most popular food to grow so it's probably appropriate that saving their seeds involves a special little project.

The accepted tomato seed saving method involves letting ripe tomatoes ferment for a few days to prevent bacterial and viral diseases from persisting through the seed. (Don't save seed from any tomato that was obviously diseased.) Fermentation also breaks down the gel that covers tomato seed.

Tomato seed saving can be a juicy ritual. Pick the tomatoes when they are really ripe. In the bottom of a pail or bucket, mush the tomatoes and squish from the pulp as many seeds as possible. (One soon finds out that cultivars vary considerably in their pulpiness.)

After you've done the mushing and squeezing, get the garden hose and add a little water so that all seeds and pulp are in the bath. Water seeds off your hands into the pail as well.

Then put a lid on and keep your bucket identified.

Three days later you'll observe a mouldy, fermented brew. (You're not supposed to let the fermenting process go on much longer.)

Begin by hosing into the liquid whatever seeds are still attached to the tomato meat. As you do this, discard most of the pulp over the side to be later composted. The pulp floats but the seeds don't. After the tomato pieces have been rinsed, pause for a few seconds as the last of the seeds sink to the bottom.

Then gently pour the liquid out of the bucket and watch all the remaining bits of skin and flesh float over the edge. Ta-dah! There are all the tomato seeds on the bottom! It can take a couple of tippings to get the liquid to come completely clear.

The next thing is to pour the clear water and the seeds onto a fine-mesh screen that collects the seeds. It's a skill to do this in one go. Usually a few seeds will be left in the pail and it will be necessary to add some more water and do another pour.

The seeds tend to clump up on the screen. A light spraying with the hose gets them evenly spread for faster drying.

The seeds dry remarkably fast. On a sunny day, if you put them on the screens in the morning, you can be storing them away in the late afternoon.

It helps to come in the middle of the day when the seeds are already mostly dry and scrape them gently off the screen with their plastic garden marker or something similar so as to aerate them a bit more. It also is a good idea to rub them between your fingers so as to separate seeds that are stuck together.

Whew. All the above is not necessarily the only way to save tomato seed. If you don't want to go the fermentation route, you could scoop a few seeds out of your homegrown tomato and put them on a plate to dry.

The seeds turn a very light colour when dry. They look and feel dry. Tomato seeds, like lettuce seeds, can be stored in small containers. They too remain viable for four or five years.

Tomato
(*Solanum lycopersicum*)

I've rarely come across tomato crosses but I know other gardeners who have seen plenty. For purity's sake, you should separate tomato varieties by at least 10 feet (3 m).

BEANS

These include regular pinto and chili beans, fresh green and yellow snap beans, peas, chickpeas, soybeans and lentils. Depending on variety, these dry down from July to October. It's best to grow cultivars that will dependably mature dry beans year after year in your garden.

In the process of drying down, all these legumes lose their leaves until only the pods are left. Most get to the point where the beans rattle in the pods if you shake them. Some bean pods twist open and spurt their seeds on hot days, so it's important to do daily checks when harvest is close. If your thumbnail can't make a dent in the seed, the beans are ready.

Pick the pods by hand, gather them in appropriate containers and take them to your drying space. Spread them onto screens or trays. Although they could be threshed immediately, giving them another drying day or two is good in case some seeds are not quite done. They dry better in the pod.

Opening the pods one by one can be a very exciting as well as mesmerizing activity.

There are lots of ways to get large amounts of beans out of their pods. I find the simplest, most efficient method is to thresh them in my wooden threshing box. Depodding them in the threshing box is a quick and fun affair. It's mostly a stepping process with the occasional shuffle to make sure you get all of them. Bean seeds could also be threshed with your feet on any hard surface using a tarp or a burlap bag. If you're stomping the beans to thresh them and not doing it by hand, it's crucial that the beans be very dry.

There are various ways of cleaning the beans at this point. You could simply pick out the beans. You could separate pod parts from seeds easily and efficiently with the right screens. You could also put beans and debris in a bucket of water; viable beans will sink and everything else will float. With this last method, the beans would need to dry out on screens again. Because I clean large volumes of seeds, I use an air compressor and squirt the chaff away using a blow nozzle attachment.

It most cases, it's probably unnecessary to give the beans additional drying time after threshing and cleaning, but it's a good precautionary measure. Having the seeds on the screens facilitates the removal of broken, munched, chipped or otherwise suspect beans. It's easy to spot beans that aren't quite finished drying: they are slightly larger and their colours aren't as deep.

It's wise to keep identifying sticks or markers with each variety at each step. When they are put away, they should get a label and date on their container.

If beans are adequately dry, freezing temperatures will not endanger their viability. On the other hand, freezing temperatures kill any insects that have managed to hitchhike rides with the seeds.

Having your own dry beans on hand means special meals are around the corner. You're unlikely to find beans in a store that have the eating quality of your homegrown ones. As seed, beans will easily stay viable for four or five years, but as food they are best eaten by next year's harvest.

Lentil (*Lens culinaris*)

You can occasionally get surprise seeds with regular dry beans and it's hard to know whether a cross has occurred or it's a genetic throwback. Such beans can be most interesting to grow out because sometimes they will continue to produce more unexpected colours and patterns. You can lessen the already remote chances of such offerings by alternating bean rows by maturity dates or with other crops. Personally, I'd rather have the occasional bean surprise to possibly grow out again.

The maintenance of seed purity is a most interesting topic for seed savers and will be discussed at the end of this chapter.

There are three kinds of beans that, because of their more open flowers, can be pollinated by insects as well as by themselves: runner beans, fava beans and lima beans. To maintain purity in these bean families, it is best to grow only one variety of each (which most people would ordinarily do anyway) or to separate them as much as possible.

Runner and fava beans appreciate a cooler growing season than regular beans and the seeds ripen unevenly over many weeks. Soybeans need three months of warm weather to dry down in late September. In North America there's hardly any awareness of significant variety differences in soybeans, fava and runner beans. These seeds have enormous potential as whole food crops.

GRAINS

Grains are self-pollinating annuals that are rarely grown out by gardeners let alone seed savers. They are one of the easiest crops to grow. Eaten as whole foods they have great potential to provide us with more healthy diets. The way things now stand, our commercial varieties are bred to be used in food products, not as food. Many important varieties will be lost if we don't become their custodians.

Grains such as barley, wheat, oats, triticale, spelt, emmer and kamut can be planted in the fall or spring depending on the severity of your winter. They usually ripen in the summer and their seed heads make wonderful music as they dance in the wind.

Gathering grain seed is a matter of cutting or pinching off the tops. As with beans, grains are ready when you can't make a dent in them with your fingernail.

Some grains have hair-like awns sticking out of the seeds that may stick to you if you brush against them. These awns, in different colours and lengths depending on the cultivar, add a lot of grace and beauty to the grain display. They need to be rubbed loose from the grains, preferably after the grains have dried another day or two on trays. I recommend using gloves because the awns are quite bristly.

Wheat
(*Triticum aestivum*)

Hulls contain the grains themselves. In some varieties these hulls can be removed by rubbing and in others the hulls are practically impossible to remove without threshing machinery. If you're saving the

Oat (*Avena sativa*)

grain for seed and not for eating, it's no matter if the hulls stay on. If stored in dry, cool conditions, grains stay viable for many years.

PEPPERS

Peppers are treated as self-pollinating annuals although they are perennials in warm climates. Most peppers ripen to a rich red. A few fruits will supply seed for hundreds of plants. Remove the seed mass, rub it to separate the seed and allow to air dry. Alternately, wash the seed with water in an appropriate container; the debris will float and the seeds can be dried again by spreading them out in the sun or in a warm place indoors.

Although peppers are self-pollinating, cross-pollination does sometimes occur. If you grow a sweet pepper and a hot pepper beside each other, you might occasionally be surprised to find your sweet pepper has some heat. Separate different pepper varieties as much as you can or grow only one variety for seed. Pepper seeds remain viable for at least four years.

The above self-pollinating annuals are an excellent place to start seed saving. Lettuces, tomatoes, beans, grains and peppers can be used in lots of meals! Cross-pollinated annuals are only a little more complicated.

CROSS-POLLINATED ANNUALS

For cross-pollinated plants, it is important to maintain variety vigour by saving seed from at least several individual plants of the same variety, even if you need only a few seeds. Saving seed from only one or two plants, known as inbreeding, reduces genetic contributions and results in reduced health and yield in succeeding generations. (Exceptions to this rule are squashes and pumpkins, which do not noticeably lose vigour even if inbred for several generations.)

BROCCOLI

Broccoli is normally cross-pollinated by bees, so it is best to grow only one variety or isolate two or more varieties considerably. For annual broccoli, an early spring sowing is recommended.

Broccoli, as a member of the *Brassica* family, will cross with cabbage, Brussels sprouts, cauliflower, collards, kale and kohlrabi, so watch not to let it flower at the same time as any of these. (This is unlikely to happen unless you are also saving seed of one or more of them.)

Broccoli
(*Brassica oleracea* Italica Gp)

Like other brassicas, broccoli seed is borne in narrow pods. Harvest the pods when they are dry and brittle. Threshing can be done by hand. The right screen makes cleaning the seed a snap. The chaff can also be blown away with a fan or hair dryer.

CORN

Corn is cross-pollinated by the wind so isolation is essential. Any one corn (sweet, ornamental, dent, flint, flour or popcorn) will cross very easily with any other, and a neighbour's corn should be at least a quarter mile (0.4 km) away. Late and early varieties can be planted beside each other if the first variety sheds its pollen before the silks appear on the second. Harvest the cobs when they are dry and give them additional drying under cover. Husks of six to eight ears can be tied together and hung in an airy place. When seeds are sufficiently dry, it is usually easy to hold an ear in one hand and twist off the kernels in another. The kernels can also be left on the cobs to be displayed through the winter. Storage life is only a year or two.

Because corn is such an inbreeder, most sources recommend growing many plants to ensure genetic diversity.

Sweet corn
(*Zea mays* convar. *saccharata* var. *rugosa*)

CUCUMBERS

Cucumbers are pollinated mainly by bees. They cross with one another but don't cross with other vine crops. Let the fruits ripen past the edible stage, when they will become golden, yellow or white. It doesn't matter if the vines are killed by frost. Slice the fruits in half lengthwise and scoop the pulp and seeds into a non-metallic container. Leave the mixture in a warm place and stir it a few times daily. Fermentation will reduce the jelly-like pulp around each seed to a thin liquid and will be complete in three or four days. The best seeds will sink to the bottom of the container and the lighter, inferior ones will rise to the top. Pour off the floating seeds, wash those remaining by stirring them in a few changes of water or washing them in a sieve, and then spread them on wax paper or screens. Dry them outdoors in sunny weather or in a warm airy room, stirring periodically to encourage uniform drying, until they feel rough but not slippery to the touch.

Cucumber (*Cucumis sativus*)

SQUASH AND PUMPKINS

Squash and pumpkins are also pollinated by bees. The four different species of squash and pumpkins won't cross species or cross with cucumbers and melons. *Cucurbita pepo* includes all common summer squashes, all acorn types, the orange pumpkin types, Delicata, Lady Godiva and Spaghetti. *Cucurbita maxima* includes Buttercup, Hubbard, Delicious, Banana and Hokkaido. *Cucurbita moschata* includes butternut and cheese types. *Cucurbita mixta* includes the cushaw squashes. All will cross with their own species members.

Fastening paper bags over the female flowers, then dabbing pollen from male flowers onto the female and closing the bag again until the chance of cross-pollination is over ensures genetic integrity. For starters, grow a representative of one or more species each growing season.

Summer squash must be left on the vine about eight weeks past its normal harvesting date until the skin becomes as hard as that of winter squash. All squash and pumpkin seeds will gain vigour if

Pumpkin (*Cucurbita pepo*)

allowed to ripen longer in the fruit. Removing and storing them can wait for a month or two. They may be left past the first fall frost.

Cut the fruit of the mature pumpkin or squash in half. Remove the seeds and moist material around them with a large spoon, place it all in a large bowl, add some water and work the mixture through your fingers. The seeds will separate gradually. Wash them again and spread them out on wax paper or screens to dry for a week or more, moving them about daily so they don't remain in small wet piles. Cull out any flat seeds; only the plump ones are viable.

If storing in a sealed jar, check them after a few weeks to see if there is any sign of moisture. If so, take them out for additional drying.

SPINACH

Spinach has very fine pollen that can be carried a mile (1.6 km) or more by the wind. Remove plants that bolt to seed without producing good spinach. Spinach seed normally ripens unevenly in the latter part of summer. Strip mature seeds from the stalks with your hands.

AMARANTH AND QUINOA

Amaranth and quinoa are cross-pollinated annuals that are often mistakenly called grains. They will cross with their wild relatives, so it is important to weed out red-rooted pigweed and lamb's quarters if you want to maintain pure seed. Amaranth cultivars will cross with each other, as will quinoa cultivars, so grow only one kind of each or separate cultivars by as much distance as you can. Certain varieties, such as purple-leaved amaranth, are easier to select for than others. Lamb's quarters has a greater branching habit than quinoa and smaller flower heads.

Amaranth is one of a very few seeds to harvest while plants are still flowering. It is more practical and efficient to get amaranth seeds before the plants die down.

Amaranth keeps going until hit by the first hard frost. Seed will often ripen many weeks before that, usually after about three months. The best way to determine if seed is harvestable is to briskly shake or rub the flower heads between your hands and see if seeds fall readily. An easy way to gather ripe amaranth is, during dry weather, to bend the plants over a bucket and rub the seed heads between your hands.

Purple-leaved amaranth
(*Amaranthus cruentus*)

On a larger scale, you can carefully stack bunches of cut flower heads, then rub them through screening into a large container or wheelbarrow. Cutting and hanging plants to dry indoors does not work very well with amaranth: the plants become extremely bristly and reluctant to release seeds.

Harvesting fresh seed from still-flowering plants means seeds still have drying to do. It's most important to further dry your crop to ensure it won't mould in storage. I usually leave amaranth seeds on trays for two or three hot days, stirring occasionally until they are as dry as possible. Store seed in tight containers in a cool, dry place.

Quinoa, a plant similar to amaranth in many ways, is harvested like most other crops. It is ready to pick when the leaves have fallen, leaving just the dried seed heads. Seeds can be easily stripped upward off the stalk with a gloved hand.

Quinoa is adapted to conditions of such low moisture that, if rained on, the mature seed can germinate. It's best to harvest quinoa just a little early if it is almost ready and extended rainfall is forecast.

Amaranth and quinoa have a very high-quality nutritional profile but the machinery of industrial agriculture does not efficiently harvest them. They have enormous potential for small-scale sustainable agriculture.

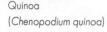

Quinoa
(*Chenopodium quinoa*)

CROSS-POLLINATED BIENNIALS

Cross-pollinated biennials produce their edible crop the first season and their flowers and seeds the second season. Since they need winter to complete their cycle, they can be left in the ground or brought indoors, depending on location and preference.

Plant seed of biennial root crops early enough that the plants will be mature at the end of the growing season. When digging up plants for storage, choose healthy plants that show characteristics desirable to the variety. Don't save seed from plants that bolt to seed the first season.

It is beneficial to prepare roots for storage by curing. This is a process that dries and toughens the skin but still leaves the root firm and plump. Curing enables the root to resist moulding and heals small breaks in the skin that would otherwise invite decay. Harvest the roots on a dry day, when the soil isn't too wet. Gently shake or rub off any excess earth. Cut the tops off about an inch (2.5 cm) above the crown and then lay them to dry, either in the sun for a few hours or indoors for a day or so. Turn them once so that all parts are exposed to air.

BEETS

Beets are cross-pollinated by the wind. The pollen is very light and can be carried long distances, so it is best to raise seed of only one variety each year. If you bring your beets indoors, pull them in the fall before heavy frosts. Cut their tops an inch (2.5 cm) above the crown. Handle beets carefully since damaged ones may rot. Three beets are adequate for most needs.

Your storage system should provide even moisture to prevent the beets from shrivelling. A storage temperature of 40°F–50°F (4°C–10°C) favours subsequent seed stalk production more than a temperature closer to freezing. A good storage method is to layer beets in a box between dampened sand or fresh sawdust.

We always leave our beets in the ground over winter and protect them from frost with a thick layer of mulch.

In the second year, beets should be thinned or replanted to about two feet (60 cm) apart, the crowns even with the soil surface. In summer, when plants are completely dry, brown mature seeds are easily stripped by hand from the branches.

Chioggia beet
(*Beta vulgaris* subsp. *vulgaris* Conditiva Gp)

As with just about any seed crop, you'll be amazed by how many seeds are produced by one plant. Beet seeds are actually seed balls, each containing up to six seeds.

SWISS CHARD

Swiss chard produces seed stalks similar to beets. Beets and Swiss chard will cross with each other, so avoid saving seeds from both crops in the same season. (That doesn't prevent you from growing both for food.) Swiss chard is extremely hardy and, for seed saving purposes, there is usually no need to dig up and store the plants.

CARROTS

Carrots are cross-pollinated by a variety of insects. They will cross readily with Queen Anne's lace, so it's important to keep this wild plant clipped so as not to flower when carrot does. Carrots and parsnips do not cross.

Carrots can be harvested in the fall before the ground freezes, leafy tops cut to one inch (2.5 cm), and stored at high humidity and near-freezing temperatures. Some people cut off only the crown or top inch (2.5 cm) of the plant for replanting. Carrots can be kept in boxes of damp sand or sawdust. In the spring, replant a foot (30 cm) apart.

In mild areas carrots can be left in the ground under thick mulch. In cold areas they will often survive outside under heavy snow cover.

Carrots grow up to six feet (180 cm) high the second year. Each has a large head with a series of branches beneath it. The flower heads are given the name "umbel" to describe flower clusters in which stalks nearly equal in length spring from a common centre. Seed umbels mature unevenly; it's best to harvest when secondary heads have ripe brown seed and third-order heads are starting to turn brown. This is usually around September of the second year. Heads can be removed as they mature or entire stalks can be cut and cured for a few weeks. Rub off seeds when completely dry and use a screen to remove the chaff.

Carrot umbels

LEEKS

Leeks are pollinated by honeybees. They may cross with onions. Generally they overwinter well. Early tall-stemmed summer types should be hilled up with soil or mulched heavily. Weed out and eat the less desirable plants in the fall. The second year individual plants will send up single stalks four feet to five feet (120 cm to 150 cm) high capped by beautiful, huge umbels composed of hundreds of flowers. In the fall, when you see the seeds inside their capsules, pick the heads and further dry them well. Brisk rubbing will extract the seeds.

ONIONS

Onions are also pollinated by honeybees and cross with each other. Harvest them as normal in fall and weed out double onions and those with thick necks. Larger bulbs will produce more seed. Prepare your onions for storage by curing them as you do your eating onions. Check that the neck area, where the tops join the bulb, is shriveled and well dried. The best storage conditions are dry, airy and cool. Be careful not to bruise or injure the bulbs, and replant them as early in spring as possible. In mild areas, and especially with sweet onions that don't store well, it is better to leave the plants in the soil over winter. Cover the bulb, leaving its top barely exposed.

Large flower heads above three-foot to four-foot (90 cm to 120 cm) stalks develop over several weeks in

Leek
(*Allium ampeloprasum* Leek Gp)

summer. Start harvesting when the fruits open to expose the black seed. Cut off the umbels as they become ready and dry them in trays or bags, on screen or canvas, in sun or under cover, stirring them occasionally. Seed should dry to the point where it is easily rubbed from the heads. Drying will often take over two weeks. Seed life is only a year or two.

PARSNIPS

Parsnips are hardy cross-pollinated biennials that are usually planted in the spring in cold climates and in mid-summer in mild areas. As with carrots, you can choose to replant only the crowns. The mature seed is dry and light brown by the next summer and shatters or falls off the plant readily, so harvest should not be delayed.

BRASSICAS

The other main cross-pollinated biennials are brassicas. Brussels sprouts, cabbage, collards, cauliflower, kale and kohlrabi are all members of the cabbage family that, like broccoli, are pollinated mainly by bees and cross-pollinate readily. They require isolation from other family members and from other varieties of themselves for true seed. Unlike (most) broccoli, they must be overwintered outside or taken into storage conditions of high humidity and near-freezing temperatures. When replanted in spring, plants should be set two to three feet (60 to 90 cm) apart. For cabbages, it is common practice to make crosscuts about an inch (2.5 cm) deep into the top centre of each head to facilitate emergence of the seed stalk. Staking keeps cabbages, which grow to five feet (150 cm) the second year, from falling over. In cold climates, cauliflower is the most difficult of the cabbage family to raise for seed because most varieties do not overwinter well either by indoor storage or by thick mulching outdoors.

Kohlrabi
(*Brassica oleracea* Gongylodes Gp)

Pods of all the brassicas burst open as they become dry and brittle. Harvesting them a little early and curing them further in paper bags or on trays after harvest is a good way to avoid losing any seed. Storage life of brassica seed is about five years.

White cabbage
(*Brassica oleracea* Capitata Gp)

Cauliflower
(*Brassica oleracea* Botrytis Gp)

PERENNIALS

For seed saving purposes, there aren't many perennial vegetables, but it's worth mentioning chives, asparagus and rhubarb.

CHIVES

Chives are pollinated by bees. They don't cross with onions or leeks.

Cut off the seed heads when the seeds blacken. Allow to further dry for a few weeks, then rub off the seeds with your hands.

ASPARAGUS

Asparagus is usually grown from the roots or crowns but can also be grown from seed. The seed is ready to harvest in the fall, when the asparagus berries turn red and the ferny top leaves flop over.

Cut asparagus tops off and hang to dry. Soak the berries in water for an hour until you can remove the pulp easily from the seed. Spread the seed on a tray and keep in a warm, dry, airy place until thoroughly dry.

RHUBARB

Rhubarb is usually grown from root sections of established plants. Not many varieties produce seed heads. The large seed disks of those that do can be gathered and dried in the usual ways.

CLONAL REPRODUCTION

With plants that reproduce clonally, seeds are not involved. Nevertheless, gardeners and farmers have the choice of maintaining these for future plantings.

Potatoes, sunroot (also called Jerusalem artichokes) and garlic are saved through their tubers or bulbs. The genetic makeup of a cultivated variety of any of these stays the same, although they can demonstrate quite different adaptations to soil and locale. Most people know there are lots of different kinds of potatoes but few realize there are dozens of distinct sunroot and garlic cultivars that vary in taste, appearance and productivity.

POTATOES

Potato plants sometimes produce seeds but they normally are of no use to the seed saver since they will not produce true. (It's fun to experiment, though.) Choose only healthy plants and undamaged tubers for reproduction because it is particularly easy for diseases to be passed on from one generation to the next. A few hours of drying outside toughens the skins for storage. How well potatoes keep doesn't seem to be affected by washing or not washing them. Burying them in dry sand is an excellent storage method. They should be kept in the dark.

Potato
(*Solanum tuberosum*)

SUNROOT

Sunroot tubers start forming with the onset of cold weather in September or October and keep growing after the visible plant has blackened and died. Sunroots are most delicious after the first frosts hit them and remain so until sprouting begins in spring. They are tricky to store because their thin skin causes them to shrivel easily. It is best to simply leave them in the ground until you want to use them, either for food or "seed."

It is advisable to start digging inward at over a foot (30 cm) beyond the stalk to avoid mutilating the tubers, which grow on lateral shoots. Sunroots are notorious for being able to sprout new growth from even the tiniest pieces of themselves.

GARLIC

We are often asked if our "seed" garlic can be eaten as well as planted. Of course, food stock and seed stock are more or less the same thing, although we do save our biggest bulbs for planting, both for our customers and for ourselves.

Except for eating purposes, garlic is out of the ground for only three or four months a year: it is usually harvested in late July and replanted in October. Not much can go wrong in those few months between harvest and replanting if you dry bulbs well after digging them. There is one thing to note, however. It used to be common practice to dry ("cure") garlic on the ground in the sun. Nowadays, because of climate change, garlic left exposed to the sun can literally cook and become translucent. So it's best to hang garlic to cure in an airy but shaded place.

Garlic (*Allium sativum*)

Garlic keeps better in bulbs than separated into cloves, so wait until shortly before planting to take the bulbs apart.

FLOWERS AND HERBS

Flowers and herbs go to seed in numerous ways. It's sometimes fascinating to figure out exactly where the seeds are, as well as the most efficient way of harvesting them. Usually seeds can be shaken or stripped by hand into a bucket. At times you have to get there before the birds or the wind.

Most garden flowers are cross-pollinated by insects. If you wish to preserve the purity of a certain strain for seed saving, grow only one variety at a time, stagger plantings considerably or set up appropriate insect barriers.

Marigold
(*Calendula officinalis*)

GENERAL HARVEST NOTES

Seeds of most plants dry right down in field or garden. If maturity is looking dubious because of the weather or if birds are significantly munching on the seeds, you can dig up entire plants and bring them indoors to complete their drying. As long as the crop is close to maturity, the seeds will continue to ripen.

It is a good rule of thumb to let harvested seed dry for at least a few more days after being removed from the plant. The larger the seed, the longer the drying period required. Most seeds will dry adequately for home storage if spread on wax paper, newspapers, trays, plates or screens in an airy place for a few days to a week. They should be turned and spread several times during that period.

An equally good drying method is to let the seed heads or stalks dry in open paper bags for one or two weeks. The drying process can be hastened by spreading the seed in a sun-exposed room, in a non-humid greenhouse or in the sun outside if they are covered or brought in at night. Lacking sun and/or greenhouse, you can speed up drying with gentle heat so long as the temperature never rises above 100°F (38°C).

GENERAL STORAGE NOTES

Seed should always be stored under cool, dry conditions. Temperatures well below freezing will not harm seeds if they have been adequately dried. Sealing most seeds from air—except in the case of beans and peas, which like some air circulation—prolongs viability.

Most sound vegetable seeds, if stored properly, will remain viable for many years, with the exception of short-lived onion, leek, corn and parsnip seed.

Put each kind of seed into its own envelope with the cultivar name and the date of storage. You can also put envelopes or just the seeds in airtight tins, glass jars or plastic containers that can be closed to make them moisture proof.

Storing seed containers in the freezer will increase longevity.

SELECTION CRITERIA

People without sophisticated training have been successfully saving seeds for the past 10,000 years. It is ironic that people with so-called scientific backgrounds are creating the possible annihilation of seeds as we've known them.

The most sought-after trait for corporate researchers these days is the ability of plants to withstand applications of poisons produced by their bosses.

On the other hand, many gardeners simply want to preserve their long-time favourite vegetables. Some growers also want to improve their crops. Nearly everyone has a different concept of what is ideal. Depending on needs and preferences, criteria for selection may include any of the following: flavour; size; lateness or earliness to bolt; trueness to type; colour; shape; thickness of flesh; hardiness; storability; and resistance to disease, drought and/or insects. It's a matter of tuning in what's important to you.

Clearly, the needs and preferences of a backyard urban gardener would be totally different from those of a 1,000-acre (400 ha) farmer. For example, someone growing food in a city would most likely prefer pole beans or climbing peas to bush beans or peas because they make maximum use of vertical space. Climbing beans and peas are crops that are not researched by governments or corporations, yet they could be grown in potentially millions of city plots.

Industrial agriculture prefers crops that ripen all at once, such as hybrid broccoli, whereas heritage broccolis that ripen unevenly are more appropriate for family and community gardens. Many seeds that are not efficiently harvested by gigantic combines, such as favas, amaranth and quinoa, can be very efficiently harvested by hand.

The yield of most savable heritage seeds is considerably less than it used to be because companies simply don't spend time with less lucrative non-hybrids. This could be changed in a few years if amateur seed savers started selecting seed from their most productive plants.

At Salt Spring Seeds, we often select for taste, especially with beans, garlic and tomatoes. We cook three or four pots of bean varieties and compare their flavours without salt or other seasoning. For garlic and tomatoes, we usually organize raw taste tests with groups that visit us; we are usually surprised by how much consensus there is.

THE QUESTION OF PURITY

Reading the few significant seed saving books available on the market might leave you with the feeling that it is crucial to maintain genetic purity. Such responsibility need not be taken on unless you are officially preserving a named variety.

Purity is simply another quality for which you can select. Having a pure variety doesn't mean that you have a variety with better overall quality. Some of the things you can do to keep seed true have already been mentioned. You can separate varieties by distance, barriers or time, or you can grow one variety of a crop. You can also keep seed from previous years in case impurities do show up.

On the other hand, if you grow certain varieties side by side and crossing does occur, your new bean, lettuce or tomato will likely taste just as good as either parent. It might also have some useful characteristics neither parent had. (Some crosses, however, such as those between squash varieties, invariably do produce inferior offspring.)

Traditionally, agricultural societies have maintained a broad genetic base (sometimes called "landraces") for each of their crops, ensuring survival of some plants in the event of disease, pests or freak weather conditions. With extreme and unpredictable changes in the natural and social worlds, identical plants are now more vulnerable than ever. Most vulnerable of all are the monoculture crops on vast acreages across North America.

Smaller-scale farmers and gardeners, on the other hand, can be more in touch with their plants and have much greater flexibility to embrace changes as they occur. If nature is now throwing out more crosses and genetic sports than ever, we should receive the message and seize the exciting opportunity to grow out such plants. Not only are we already blessed with all the plants we need to feed the planet, there are many more that are continually being offered for our nourishment and enjoyment.

AESTHETIC DIMENSIONS OF SEED SAVING

Seed saving not only lightens our living on the land by grounding us in the reality of what completes the circle of growing, but also enhances and beautifies the garden in configurations of maturing plants that have yet to be explored in gardening books and catalogues.

Some common vegetables, such as onions, leeks, lettuces, endives, kales and chicories, become very different when they flower and then go to seed. Leaves change shape, stalks shoot skyward, flowers contrast with foliage, seed heads explode into reality; plants become hardly recognizable as the vegetables you were eating. As you get to know the colours, shapes and sizes to expect, you can choose varieties for specific effects, incorporating your seed plants into overall garden design.

There are also the unplanned combinations that appear from plants saved for seed! Seeds often escape the seed saver's attempts to collect them all. Volunteer plants of favourite vegetables and flowers may pop up in new places. Sometimes these volunteers appear even earlier than greenhouse sowings, and usually they are more vigorous and better adapted than pampered transplants. Often they locate themselves in spots that delight the eye and warm the heart. Ever more beautiful gardens can come from learning to anticipate and play with such gratuitous offerings.

PART 4

Seed Saving in Communities

I THINK WE LIVE in a time when it is crucially important to save seeds with family, friends and neighbours. If we don't, we may soon see the day when our seeds are gone. It's already true that many people don't eat whole food anymore, only packaged, processed food.

Just a few decades ago, our seeds were a public resource. It's the right time now for us as the public to get our seeds back to being the storehouses of healthy food they used to be.

In this regard, a lot is already happening.

SEEDY SATURDAYS

Seedy Saturdays are one of the most radical initiatives to keep our heritage of seeds alive. An annual seedy event that usually happens on a Saturday in late winter, it brings together all the people in a community who are excited by seeds.

The first Seedy Saturday was in Vancouver, British Columbia, in 1990 and was organized by Sharon Rempel and Roy Forster. Carolyn Herriot coordinated the second one in Victoria, BC, in 1996. Now Seedy Saturdays have germinated in dozens of communities, towns and cities across Canada. They are very enjoyable events that help preserve and enhance plant varieties that stand out in any particular place. Seedy Saturdays provide great opportunities to find out more about seed saving. They create an informal network of people who know how to save the seeds of what grows best in an area.

It is very easy to organize a Seedy Saturday (or a Seedy Sunday or a Seedy Monday night... or to have one after harvest as well as one in spring). All you have to do is rent a hall, find a big living room or set up in a barn. Put up posters, have a story in the local paper, announce it at community meetings.

Most Seedy Saturdays have a big swap table where people can easily look over the seeds that have been contributed. But one doesn't necessarily have to make a rule of this. Everybody with seeds could have their own table or everyone could just walk around with their seeds, talking and trading. Having knowledgeable volunteers at an exchange table makes things a lot more informative for neophyte growers.

It's helpful to have a classification system such as signs indicating areas of herbs, flowers, veggies, perennials, potatoes, garlic, etc. It's also good to have as much signage as possible about the seed offerings. Some people bring their seeds in seed packets with written descriptions and some people bring jars or bags of their seeds. Remember to have lots of empty coin envelopes as well as a few scoops and spoons.

Many Seedy Saturdays are large events with tables representing gardening clubs, local seed companies, conservancy groups, alternative energy advocates, etc. Display tables can have seed saving equipment and information. Catalogues of companies and organizations promoting heirloom seeds can be available for perusal. Beverages, snacks or meals can be made from locally grown heritage crops.

Participating in an annual seed exchange may profoundly alter your garden planning in the friendliest of ways. You might end up growing something for someone that does particularly well for you in exchange for something that doesn't. You might come to depend on certain seedy friends to provide you with certain seeds. As a group, you might be able to figure out how to maximize seed production in your neighbourhood.

FAMILY, FRIENDS AND NEIGHBOURS

With family, friends and neighbours, simple trading of seeds can happen anytime or any way that's convenient.

This is nothing new but it could be happening a lot more. As gardeners realize they can save seeds and don't have to depend on seed companies for them, their empowered feeling will become contagious. Because every grower has personal favourites, swapping seeds is a natural way for high-quality seeds to get around.

Trading seeds with your Aunt Thelma halfway across the country creates seed security in these weird years when one season can have record heat and another record cold. She might be able to give you corn seed this time around, but it may be your turn to help her next. If Thelma's ex is also trading seeds with both of you, then it's even more likely that someone (and thus everyone) will have corn seed.

One of the great things about maintaining seed varieties among a circle of people is that, barring crop failures, you need only one member to grow lettuces, tomatoes or peppers to ensure everyone's seed supply. Such is nature's seed bounty that one lettuce, one tomato and one pepper from that one person theoretically could provide everyone's seeds, with some left over. When you consider that lettuce, tomato and pepper seeds easily stay viable for five years, it becomes obvious how simple it can be for a small group of people to keep lots of seeds alive.

As with Seedy Saturdays, there are many ways of organizing your exchanges, depending on who and where you are. You could visit each other, mail each other seeds (seeds are so light!), set it all up at conference calls, pass on the word with email, make a four-year plan, unite parts of the family here and there.

You could each have certain varieties for which you are responsible or you could alternate varieties. You could all be tomato seed savers.

You could make evaluations and selections in addition to sharing zeal.

Gardeners make these connections naturally. In our local post office, no one ever decided to make it happen; nevertheless six women employees have been trading fruits, vegetables, flowers, plants, cuttings and seeds for many years.

SEED ORGANIZATIONS

There are national seed organizations in Canada and the United States that research, catalogue, preserve and distribute "heritage" or "heirloom" seeds.

Having been involved with these groups over the years in addition to selling old varieties through Salt Spring Seeds, I have observed recent changes in the meaning of "heirloom" or "heritage."

Until a few decades ago, everyone seemed to agree that such seeds had to have been around 50 years or more to merit the title. But now, our entire heritage of seeds is, in fact, being threatened by corporate seeds that you can't save. Up until the 1990s, many excellent open-pollinated varieties were developed by companies and governments working to improve crops (instead of to resist herbicides or to grow well with high chemical inputs). These cultivars are as worthy of saving as their older parents and are coming to be regarded as heirlooms too.

Similarly, it is important to note that the meaning of "hybrid" has changed. Fifty years ago, hybrids were the result of simple crosses that either happened spontaneously in nature or were facilitated by gardeners or researchers. Such hybrids were stabilized by growing them out over a number of seasons, after which you could expect to get the same variety year after year by saving seed. Now hybrids refer to plant cultivars with parent lines controlled by plant breeders. Such varieties have not been stabilized and their seed is mostly worthless for seed saving purposes. It is necessary to go back to the seed company for such hybrid seed.

Thus, the seeds that you can obtain from heritage seed exchanges aren't necessarily very old, but they are all open-pollinated or non-hybrid, in the modern sense of the word. Seeds come true and members are encouraged to save them.

The vitality of these organizations is dependent on the number of members not only growing out seeds but re-offering them as well. The seed saver organizations in Canada and the United States send all members an annual descriptive listing of who has seeds and who wants seeds. No fee is charged except to cover postage. Through their publications, members of these groups learn not only about seed saving but also about heritage gardens, seed companies and the stories of heirloom cultivars. These organizations maintain and formalize our living legacy of diverse plant resources:

Seeds of Diversity Canada: #1–12 Dupont St. West, Waterloo, ON, N2L 2X6; www.seeds.ca Seeds of Diversity Canada maintains on its website a list of companies that sell heirloom, rare or endangered varieties of vegetables, fruits, flowers and herbs.

Seed Savers Exchange: 3076 North Winn Rd.,
Decorah, IA, 52101, USA; www.seedsavers.org

SEED COMPANIES

Some companies in Canada and the United States still specialize in open-pollinated seeds. Salt Spring Seeds has traded seeds with many of these companies over the years and I have delighted in the spirit of openness and cooperation that has always permeated the exchanges.

In 1999, a coalition of seed companies came together out of concern for the potential risks associated with the use of genetic engineering. Member seed companies, including Salt Spring Seeds, endorse the following Safe Seed Pledge:

> Agriculture and seeds provide the basis upon which
> our lives depend. We must protect this foundation
> as a safe and genetically stable source for future gen-
> erations. For the benefit of all farmers, gardeners
> and consumers who want an alternative, we pledge
> that we do not knowingly buy or sell genetically
> engineered seeds or plants. The mechanical transfer
> of genetic material outside of natural reproductive
> methods and between genera, families or kingdoms
> poses great biological risks as well as economic,

political and cultural threats. We feel that genetically engineered varieties have been insufficiently tested prior to public release. More research and testing are necessary to further assess the potential risks of genetically engineered seeds. Further, we wish to support agricultural progress that leads to healthier soils, genetically diverse agricultural ecosystems and ultimately healthy people and communities.

How likely are you to find GMO seed in a garden seed catalogue these days? Fortunately, the answer still is "very unlikely." This contrasts with the extreme likelihood of obtaining food products derived from gene-altered seeds. So far, most development and planting of bioengineered crops has been with corn, canola and soybeans (and cotton as a non-food crop). Vast acreages are being grown with these and, if you look at the label on any packaged food in the supermarket, you'll find it virtually impossible to buy something that doesn't contain some form of them. GMO alfalfa, papaya, sugar beet, summer squash and potatoes are also being grown.

If you start seeing gene-modified seed in catalogues, it will be much more expensive than regular seed. You could tell your favourite seed companies you'd be more likely to remain a customer if they didn't go in for biotech seeds.

GARDENING MAGAZINES

There used to be only two or three gardening magazines on our local newsstands but now there are two or three dozen. Quite a few of these have started providing a seed exchange section where subscribers list seeds they are offering or requesting.

SEEDY INDIVIDUALS

Individual seed savers can make a huge difference with their own initiatives. Farmers' markets are great venues for turning people on to heritage seeds and plants. Grocery stores and markets can be convinced to carry heirloom, open-pollinated plants. You can generate substantial income by being the one to grow these potted plants. Providing descriptions and background as well as taste samples adds to the excitement and to the sales.

Through the simple process of selecting for desired traits, plant lovers can improve our old cultivars. It used to be that seed companies did such selection as a matter of course. Now most seed companies are primarily seed merchants that buy seed stock from the big boys who see little profit in improving simple, savable seeds.

I would strongly encourage you to start your own seed company if you feel the calling. There's room for many more regional seed companies.

As I hope you can see from this section, there is much going on in the world of seeds that is working toward a revitalization of our daily meals. You can help make a lot more happen.

AFTERWORD

WE LIVE IN CHALLENGING TIMES. Ecological crises, unstable markets, fuel shortages, natural disasters, social unrest, the pressures of globalization... Amid such uncertainty, how can we guarantee food security for ourselves and for our communities? We need seeds, land and people, and we need to work together.

We will have to create new ways of collaborating as we work the land. We will need many kinds of farms and gardens as well as farmers and gardeners. And of course, we will need SEEDS! We cannot grow good food without good seeds. The principles in part 4, "Seed Saving in Communities," are just the beginning.

TAKING SEEDY SATURDAYS TO THE NEXT LEVEL

To my mind, it would take only a few small steps to trans-
form Seedy Saturdays into real bastions of food security that
would enable communities not only to maintain their own
seeds but also to grow their own food.

First, the focus would need to shift from a somewhat
haphazard collection of fabulous heritage seeds to a more
judicious and balanced selection. The idea would be to round
out many crops so their diversity could be utilized and appre-
ciated throughout the seasons. For example, paste tomatoes
are probably as important as fresh-eating ones because they
can provide the sauces for beans and grains every month of
the year. Dry peas are vastly underappreciated in Canada
and the right varieties could provide the main dish for many
meals. Local grain production is beginning to catch on and
we should explore the rich possibilities of whole barleys,
wheats, oats and ryes as part of our diet.

Each community could make its own unique decisions
about what is most important to grow. People in cities, for
example, would likely opt to grow crops more suited to vertical space. Probably peppers would be more valued than
their eggplant cousins because they are higher in vitamins.
If the question is always about how best to feed ourselves
instead of how best to make money from food, the answers
will come easily.

The second important shift would be to ensure that seed savers are growing out sufficient quantities of seeds to actually feed the community. There are already a lot of certain seeds at Seedy Saturdays, but some important ones would need to be multiplied considerably. Again, each community would have to start calculating how much kale, carrots or garlic would work to feed the community. One of the miraculous things about seeds is the abundance of them produced by each plant. To take my favourite example, the seeds from a short row of amaranth could grow many miles of rows the next year.

The third important shift would be to formalize Seedy Saturdays a little more so that there are people keeping track of essential information. All the Seedy Saturdays I attend are testaments to the remarkable organizational powers of large numbers of dedicated volunteers. Communication channels are already in place. The next step would be to have accessible records of seed savers, seeds being saved and variety descriptions, and to encourage communication about all things seedy throughout the year.

With these simple ways of broadening Seedy Saturdays—deciding on the most important crops, growing more seed, keeping in communication—it becomes easy to coordinate growing efforts. I don't think that finding the land to grow food will be a problem when growing food becomes essential for survival, but having the right seeds on hand could be!

STARTING COMMUNITY SEED SANCTUARIES

Of course Seedy Saturdays aren't the only avenue to community seed security. Towns and cities can and already have started up active seed banks, and many more are taking their first steps.

There are a couple of easy ways communities can initiate ongoing seed collections of locally adapted plant varieties. One would be to dedicate a monthly meeting of the garden club to exchanging and maintaining seeds of foods and herbs. Another would be to take a proportion of the seeds that people bring to the swap table at annual Seedy Saturdays and keep them together, well documented and in a few safe places.

Our own Salt Spring Seed Sanctuary here on Salt Spring Island has been going for 18 years. We've opted to call ourselves a sanctuary instead of a bank because we consider seeds a lot holier than money.

We have a seed and information table at our annual Seedy Saturday. We keep the Salt Spring Island Garden Club informed of our activities. We also have one get-together a year when we bring the seeds we've saved for the Sanctuary.

The seeds are kept in a special facility we built for them. It's a very satisfying feeling to see all the seed containers on the shelves, grouped together by year and type of crop. We grow out most of our favourite varieties annually and try to ensure that no varieties lose their viability.

Although we have a good seed storage facility, we still consider the Sanctuary to exist in all the Salt Spring Island gardens where the foods and herbs are grown. If your community decides to save seeds together, they needn't be kept in just one place. Thanks to computers, it's easy to maintain good records of where things are.

Our Seed Sanctuary is now trying to enlist more seed savers to grow enough seeds so we can feed all our island folk. If you are interested in initiating such a project for your city or town, here are some ideas that have been working for us.

- Tell interested seed savers how easy, rewarding and important seed saving is.
- Encourage growers to take on even a single seed. It doesn't take many people to maintain a substantial amount of seed for future food choices.
- Enlist the help of experienced seed growers to serve as mentors for people beginning to save seeds.
- Divide the crops into categories such as beans, grains, greens, roots, tomatoes, potatoes, squash, corn, herbs and perennials. If there were a mentor for each, then the first-time seed saver would have to learn only about the seed saving techniques for a specific seed.
- Enlist a few adept computer people to maintain records of the seeds, the growers, the growing conditions, etc. Keep records on paper too.

- Work out arrangements with the seed growers as to how much seed they keep back and how much seed is stored in a community facility.
- Get everyone thinking about how and where to grow more food.

Being an island, Salt Spring could easily have its flow of food supplies disrupted. In these changing times, island mentality may come to cities and regions not previously considered islands. In fact, there is now a worldwide movement of cities and towns that are considering how to become more locally self-reliant. I believe Canadians can forge a new grassroots agriculture that emphasizes health and nutrition rather than profit and exploitation. People, communities and organizations can unite across this vast country of ours to weather the coming years with resilience and optimism.

PRIORITIZING PULSES

And what are the best crops to grow for food self-sufficiency and security?

For all the years I've had Salt Spring Seeds, it's always been strange to me that the crops I think are the best overall have never been glamorized as the stars they are. You'll find few of them listed in garden seed catalogues in North

America. You won't find many among the seed savers lists of Seeds of Diversity Canada or the US Seed Savers Exchange. They provide a very small part of the diet of Canadians and Americans, yet they could be contributing much more to our health and our wealth.

These crops have been around for over 8,000 years. They are the most important food in many cultures. Canada grows millions of metric tons of them annually and exports more of them than any other country. They require less energy to grow, store and prepare than most other foods. I think these long-cherished crops are the foods of the future.

I am talking about the pulses.

These are dry peas, favas, chickpeas (garbanzos), lentils and regular dry beans. They don't include fresh green beans or peas. They don't include soybeans or peanuts, which have a much higher fat content; pulses contain virtually no fat.

Pulses are miracle crops. As legumes, they increase soil fertility by taking nitrogen out of the air and putting it in the ground. They do this in association with soil organisms on their roots. By pulling a plant out of the ground, you can observe the root nodules where the nitrogen fixing takes place, which become larger and more numerous over time. I have often grown pulses in the same place for two or three years. Yields increase the second year and even more so the third year. With all the talk of renewable energy these days, pulses shine with their ability to increase soil fertility by simply growing!

Pulse plants don't require as much heat as soybeans or peanuts and are quite drought tolerant. Thus they can easily grow to maturity across Canada and in most of the northern United States. Canada exports pulses to many nations that esteem them highly, but Canadians consume less than 10 per cent of the dry peas, beans, favas, chickpeas and lentils grown in their own country. It is time to cultivate and appreciate these seeds because of the rich food security they can provide as well as the economic prosperity they can continue to bring.

The high nutritional value of pulses means they could become an important part of any healthy diet. They are rich in protein, fibre and complex carbohydrates. They contain an impressive variety of vitamins and minerals. They are recommended for heart health, diabetes and weight control and they are an excellent choice for vegetarian, vegan and gluten-free diets.

Countries around the world enjoy the diverse variety of pulses in myriad ways. A quick internet search will lead you to lots of fascinating food and seasoning combinations with special names.

Fewer herbicides and pesticides are used by industrial agriculture on pulses than on most other crops. However, they also can be grown without the use of poisons. Indeed,

I have been doing so myself for over 30 years. And so have a few hundred generations of farmers before the current one that relies on herbicides and pesticides!

To my mind, it's really crucial that we get back to organic seed and food production because everyone wants to eat safe food. Thus we need to research and rediscover the best pulses for ecological growing. Some of these are probably the same cultivars that are now being grown with poisons but that could be grown without them.

Pulses have been grown in temperate climates since the dawn of agriculture. Many civilizations evolved around diets of pulses for proteins combined with a cereal crop to provide energy. Gardeners and small-scale farmers could be doing the same in North America, and in so doing grow a very substantial part of our daily diet. On my farm, I have been harvesting about 20 pounds (9 kg) of some pulses per hundred-foot (30 m) row. City gardeners wishing to take advantage of vertical space can harvest 20 pounds (9 kg) of dry peas or beans per 50-foot (15 m) row of climbing cultivars. That's a lot of high-quality food from a small space.

Besides their ease of cultivation and their nutritional and ecological benefits, pulses are easy to store. They will keep for years if stored in tightly covered containers in a cool dark place, though it is best to prepare pulses within a year of harvest since they become drier and harder to digest over time and will require longer cooking.

Pulses are simple to prepare and they make delicious meals with minimal adornment.

In North America, we have wine, cheese, beer and chocolate experts as well as connoisseurs of tomatoes, peppers, squash, coffee, tea, meat, apples and chocolate. It's high time we praised the wonderful diversity of pulses!

Our lives depend on the seed and food choices we make. Corporations are mostly dictating those choices these days: the largest manufacturers of poisons on the planet are now also making our seeds, our food and our medicines. I'm really happy to report, however, as one whose job it is to stay connected to such things, that people and communities everywhere are starting to make their own food choices. There is a vigorous mushrooming movement that is all about wholesome food, local self-empowerment and a better relationship with the rest of life on this planet.

Seed sanctuaries, seed libraries, seed exchanges and seed initiatives are popping up across North America. There are more Seedy Saturdays and Sundays as well as lots more Community Supported Agriculture (CSA) programs. Elementary schools, high schools, colleges and universities are establishing garden plots and creating classes about sustainable agriculture. Garden clubs are featuring talks about food, herbs and local self-reliance. I keep hearing of new community gardens and orchards. It feels like something new is being born, a world in which we care for our gifts instead of obliterating them.

We can stand up for the holiness of the earth and all its wonders. We can ardently and fearlessly learn not to buy into the greed and selfishness that threatens to destroy us. We can save the good seeds that grow healthy food while loving the web of life that makes it all possible.

Each seed creates hundreds, thousands, even tens of thousands of versions of itself. We need our old seeds more than ever, not only to feed us but also to teach us, as they always have, about interconnectedness, abundance and diversity. The selves we grow will be the seeds we sow.